CONTENTS

CYCLISTS:

A Spotter's Guide

by Robbie Guillory

Illustrations by Judith Hastie

Copyright

For Fi, with thanks for everything

"One moment the bicycle would be on the gravel path, and he on top of it; the next, the position would be reversed — he on the gravel path, the bicycle on him. Now he would be standing flushed with victory, the bicycle firmly fixed between his legs. But his triumph would be short-lived. By a sudden, quick movement it would free itself, and, turning upon him, hit him sharply over the head with one of its handles."

JEROME K JEROME, THREE MEN ON THE BUMMEL

INTRODUCTION:

On Cyclists and Their Bicycles

What are the origins of the cyclist? Which came first, the bicycle or its rider? What exactly is that pump for? These are some of the questions that have vexed cycle spotters like myself for almost two hundred years.

One theory is that cyclists are a branch of a horse-riding species that proliferated until the Second World War, when demand for glue to make Spitfires and bunting saw horse numbers decline drastically.

Another theory suggests that cyclists are more closely related to cod-piece wearers of medieval times. The bicycle or 'extension' is merely decorative and 'worn' between the legs rather than ridden. These naturally became more complex and multi-functional until they evolved into a method of travelling quickly between opportunities to show off. The principal evidence to support this are the huge numbers of display-driven cyclists, or 'posing bastards', to be found in Britain today.

Marxist Cyclothologists are divided between those that believe bicycles were created by Bosses as a means of oppressing the downtrodden masses through rampant consumerism (see Gnome Chomski's *On Yer Bike: Cycling and the Capitalist Movement of Labour*) and those who suggest that they were in fact invented by workers as a means of escaping the mordant shackles of the global industrial-military complex.

Freudian Cyclothologists are known for their commitment to Mother as inventor of the bicycle, and therefore the cyclist. The act of 'mounting' and 'riding' are obvious re-creations of the Oedipal relationship, while car drivers are substitute Father-hate figures to be maligned at every opportunity.

Members of the New Age wing of Cylcothology have written extensively about how aliens (led by their leader Leonardo Da Vinci) brought bicycles to earth in the 16th Century. It took, they say, around 250 years for mankind to work out what the hell these contraptions were for (having tried and failed to utilize them as weapons, art, plumbing, musical instruments or extravagant sex aids).

In recent years there have been renewed calls for cyclists to be re-classified as vermin, so high are their concentrations on weekday commuter routes and on country roads on Sundays. I of course disagree vehemently with this stance. As a founder member of the Collaborative Opposition to Cyclist Killing Society I hope that this book will challenge readers' prejudices and misconceptions, showing just how magnificently diverse and majestic a species the cyclists of these islands are. Rather than being the scourge they're presented as in certain sections of the media, cyclists invariably exist within a fragile eco-system of online bike shops, magazines and cycle lanes that, if disturbed could see certain breeds become extinct almost instantly.

Having studied cyclists professionally for over forty years, I remain utterly fascinated by their extravagant displays, captivated by their hierarchical interactions – sometimes aggressive, sometimes collaborative – and amused by their incomprehensible behavior. I have striven, though a lifetime of empirical observation, both in the laboratory and in field conditions, to uncover the secrets of their motivations and idiosyncrasies.

I've tried wherever possible to pair particular breeds of cyclist with their most common mounts, to give young and first-time spotters assistance in quick and accurate recognition. However, as certain veterans will complain (let's face it, that's their favourite pastime), this could be misleading. Each species of cyclist, they say, can easily be seen riding any type of bicycle at any point. However, it is this spotter's belief, after years of research, that the pairings that follow are typical.

I would like to conclude with the reminder that cyclist spotting doesn't provide the instant gratification that so many seek these days; it demands patience, dedication, a willingness to travel widely and the robustness required to spend many hours outside in all weathers. However, those who are diligent will be rewarded handsomely. I hope this book encourages many new spotters, young and old, to join our ranks.

HABITATS

T he cyclist is a highly evolved creature, often only capable of surviving within very specific environments. However, across the 26 most common breeds included here, a vast range of habitats are represented, covering the length and breadth of the country. This variety demonstrates just how adaptable cyclists are.

The British Isles comprises of some 250,000 miles of road and vast swathes of still uncharted mountain-bike track. It is this cross-country network that allows cyclists to follow traditional migration patterns each year, from the highly populated southern reaches to the high mountain passes of Scotland, the waters of the Lake District, the cliff tops of Ireland's Atlantic coastline and the verdant Welsh valleys. This is not to forget the 800-odd islands along our coasts, many of which are excellent places to find the rarer species. Few home-grown cyclist-spotters consider their education complete without a visit to the unforgiving, tree-less heathlands of the Orkney and Shetland Islands, where the odd rarity from Scandinavia, blown off course, can attract thousands of twitchers.

The last half century has seen a remarkable change in population concentrations. Since 1997, and the rise of the right-on eco-leftie, the largest number of cyclists now live, like the fox, in an urban environment. This is doubtless driven by access to feeding grounds, nesting spaces, a well maintained road network and the all-important internet – source of vast reserves of 'bike-porn', vital for any cyclist's survival.

Interestingly, this soft living has made many of the urban types listed in this book overweight, mangy and over-reliant on eating out of bins. The parlous state of certain breeds, such as the *Office Magnet*, is a worry to all of us at COCKS. We're currently in consultation over plans to capture several examples and, after a period of acclimatization, re-release them in mountainous areas where they are sure to thrive. However, so they don't displace indigenous species, such as the *Mountain Ranger*, we'll also let loose some natural predators, such as the *Black Cab* (or even a ruthlessly efficient *Reversing Transit* or two – see *Predators*). That should make sure culling isn't necessary in a few years.

The final habitat covered in this book is of course the great British B-road, which is the principal reason why our country boasts such healthy populations of non-urban cyclists. What greater pleasure is there than, round a hedge-lined bend, being startled by a rising flock of Lycra-covered *Tourers*, bedecked in brilliant reds and yellows, greens and whites. However, a great threat to *Tourers* is illegal hunting. Most favoured by poachers is the Massey-Ferguson method, which is both inhumane and downright messy.

No spotter should die before they've seen wonderful sight of weary, travel-stained *Tourers* arriving from Land's End at their northern summer outpost, John O' Groats, after a grueling 700-mile migration. That they manage to find their way such a vast distance without Sat-Nav, and with the added distraction of over 5000 pubs on the way, in one of nature's great miracles. This annual migration is a sight never beaten – hundreds of *Tourers* at their very peak of their condition arriving at their destination, saying in unison, 'Is this all there is? What a dump...'

A GUIDE TO THE GUIDE

*C*yclists, a Spotter's Guide provides the essential information for spotting all breeds of cyclist. In addition I have included short notes on habitat, mating calls, usual range of travel, and other cyclists that individual breeds are most likely to flock with. We have also, where possible, provided a carefully observed drawing of a typical member of each species to aid the beginner. At the back of this book you will also see a checklist to help you log your spotting successes.

Please note, this guide only provides for species of cyclist native to the British Isles. For an excellent compendium of European cyclists this Spotter suggests Rectum-Smythe's Cyclists Abroad: *What They Look Like and How to Shoot Them* (Jockstrap Press, 1947) which, though written for a purpose any self-respecting COCK now finds barbaric, it offers great detail on all known non-native species, as well as pornographic photographs.

BE PREPARED!

There are a few items that you should always obtain before embarking on a spot of cyclothology. Luckily, none are all that expensive, and all are open to interpretation to a greater or lesser extent. Of course, spotters of all varieties enjoy a bit of kit, and, should you come to a COCKS convention in the future, you will see members who can hardly move under the weight of cyclist lures, pop-up tents, wind testing devices and the like. It is important to remember that, as in all things to do with spotting cyclists, you have a choice, and should not feel pressured into holding back some of your wages from your poor mother just so you can buy a pair of roof prism Celestron Echelon 20x70 binoculars. Housekeeping keeps your body and soul together, and you certainly can't eat fully multi-coated optics, no matter how great they are. So find below a short guide to the basics, the four pillars of cyclothology.

1.	*An anorak* – it can be wet out there, and this is the perfect all-weather item, being cool enough to wear in the summer months or over a jersey in two feet of snow (though probably pointless conditions to be spotting in!) Please try to avoid the green and brown anorak so favoured by birdwatchers, and the blue or red varieties worn by train spotters. We at COCKS have encouraged the wearing of the

	yellow anorak; it is an important display of devotion to the sport.
2.	*Notebook and guide* – such as this one. You need to have a reference to identification, and it f you aren't writing down when and where you saw that Metal Stallion then, frankly, you're not spotting.
3.	*Pencil* – many first-time spotters tend to think that any old pen will do but you could not be more wrong! Picture yourself trying to make notes about a trio of *Tourers* steadily moving up the A1/M through driving rain; the ink will run. A good B-strength graphite nib will not run, and will allow you to rub out your spots at year's end and start afresh without needing a new book!
4.	*Camera* – in this book we have taken the old-fashioned approach of using illustration (see the Note on the Illustrations) but we at COCKS fully understand the usefulness, clarity and attention to detail provided by the photograph. What is important is that you have some aide-memoire of your greatest spots. In the spring after the great winter of '62-'63 I spotted a *Russian Icebreaker* (sadly not covered in this book) ploughing through the sands of Alloa, and I will always have my postcard freehand illustration to look back on fondly, as I will certainly never see another one of those again.

The digital age has allowed the spotting community to communicate in ways unimagined in my youth. You will find several blogs and forums dedicated to the sport, as well as a number of photo-upload sites where you can display your hard-won images. Always remember to use the #COCKS hashtag when sharing a photo of a cyclist, so that we can find it!

WHAT GOES ON UNDER THE ANORAK?

B ecause cyclist spotting is an outdoor sport, I've listed below some suggested clothing standards to help you spend as much time out there as possible. If you follow these few rules you'll be filling that logbook as fast as a *Racer*!

Comfortable – you will be spending a lot of time trying to be as still as possible. A scratchy hair shirt won't be any use to you after about three minutes, no matter how warm it may be! Choose things that are easy to wear, made of soft fabrics and retaining that ever-important warm attribute!

Dull – spotters of all fields get a bad reputation for being 'uncool' but that is because we have to be (I like Maroon Five just as much as the next man). You clothing must be dull to look at, so you don't stand out and scare off flighty cyclists such as *Wobblers*.

Water and wind proof – your top half may be alright under that anorak, but what about your lower extremities? Wear thick corduroy, and ask your nan for a pair of waterproof trousers for Christmas.

Layers – it can be hot, cold, wet and then hot again, so make sure you've got a few layers to peel off or pop back on again as needed. A comfortable temperature is vital for a comfortable body, which, as point 1 says, is vital for a good day's spotting.

Large pockets – You've got large pockets on your anorak, but those will be taken up with pencil, guide book, and cyclist log, so where is your lunch going to go, eh?

NOTE ON THE ILLUSTRATIONS

As mentioned earlier, we have chosen to follow the traditional path with this book, using illustrations rather than photographs. Judith Hastie has been a keen cyclothologist for many years, and has spent a large part of that time perfecting skills that have, sadly, become neglected since the start of the photographic age. She has spent the last two years travelling the length and breadth of the British Isles, sketching from life rather than photographs, to gather in one volume our native cyclists and many of their most fearsome predators. At the next AGM she will be giving a talk of how she was almost taken for a *Wobbler* by a Canal Lurker, and also how she stayed up for three nights next to a restrained bicycle, only to discover on the morning of the fourth day that a *Thieving Bastard* had taken it!

WHY WATCH CYCLISTS?

This is a question I am often asked, and one that I have, for many years, found difficult to answer. I watch them because they are fascinating, because they are so different from us, despite looking so alike. Ever since I first read Flann O'Brien's treatise in the Third Policeman, that the cyclist evolved through a symbiotic relationship with its bicycle, I was hooked.

Cyclist are not as mindless as birds, or as artificial as trains. Cyclists are the last remaining megafauna in the British Isles, evolving after the great extinctions that heralded the arrival of man.

I love the way some varieties effortlessly power along, so silently. And I enjoy watching the less elegant ones sway about.

Everyone has their own reasons, and I'm sure you will never hear the same answer for any of the members of COCKS, but we all have two uniting characteristics: to see them all, and a burning passion for them.

HOW TO HELP WILD CYCLISTS IN YOUR STREET AND BEYOND

C yclists across the country are under threat. The rise in predator numbers (especially of *Juggernauts*), and the increase in traffic density on our roads, along with the destruction of habitats for cyclists and the effects of global warming, are creating a perfect storm that could threaten to overwhelm the delicate balance that cyclists must maintain at all times. There are a few things that we at COCKS are doing and that you at home can do to try to create space for cyclists in our modern lives.

Campaigning for more cyclist lanes is the most important thing a lover of cyclists can do. Cyclist lanes give cyclists safe passage to and from their feeding grounds, and help urban cyclists traverse the city without having to rely on dangerous, narrow streets where *Parked Menaces* lie in wait. Outside urban areas, we campaign for the creation of cyclist routes, using old train tracks, footpaths and minor B roads to establish cyclist corridors the length and breadth of the country. This not only looks after mountain and migratory cyclists, but also lets some movement happen between urban centres, to ease the pressure on isolated gene pools.

Many parks, such as the Valley Gardens in Harrogate, carry 'NO CYCLISTS' signs. This has to stop. Fledgling cyclists need somewhere to get their wheels working properly, and the rough paths in public parks and gardens are essential for getting the stabilisers worn off. These decisions are made at a local council level, and can only be changed by people living within the vicinity getting involved.

Here are a few other things that can be done at a local level:

As you will see in the section on *Predators* (see page 106), potholes aren't actively hunting cyclists, but their presence has a detrimental effect on their movements. Fill yours in with gravel or, better still, some tarmacadam.

If you live in suburbs, there is probably not a bicycle repair lair for quite some miles, so it is always good practice to leave a puncture repair kit and a bottle of chain lubricant at the gateway of your house. Not only will it help cyclists, it will also help you by attracting different cyclists to your neighbourhood. The odd high-energy gel or drink would also be welcomed.

THE OFFICE MAGNET

T he *Office Magnet* is at its most active during the early hours of the morning or during the evening, most often when the weather is clement, but its rigorous schedule is never hampered by the changing hours of daylight. A creature of habit, it rarely travels beyond the nesting grounds (often found in the suburbs of our largest cities) and its feeding ground in the metropolitan centres, where it will spend the day sifting cups of tea and coffee for biscuit crumbs.

During the summer months the *Office Magnet* can be easily identified by the small-wheeled fold-up bicycle it rides to work, pedalling furiously but going nowhere fast. Often dressed in a billowing charcoal plumage with light blue shirt, another identifying factor is that one trouser leg will be rolled up to display either a grey or a white stocking poking out of rather impractical black shoes. A grey helmet is always present, often seeming to perch atop a reddened bulbous pate.

In the depths of winter these identifying features can become rather tricky due to the darkness of the hour of flight, but with a good-strength headlamp you'll be able to pick out the poorly fitting fluorescent winter coat, and the movement of an *Office Magnet's* flickering helmet light is highly distinguishable, as it bobs wildly with each gasping breath and lunging foot. Occasionally, around the time of the 'Christmas night out' the inebriated *Office Magnet* can be seen at 2am arguing with a *Black Cab* who refuses to accommodate his cycle in the back of the taxi.

Habitat – Closely bound to the city
Range – No more than three miles from the nest
Voice – Often obscured by the noise of general traffic, a rather dispiriting wheeze
Comfortable around – *New Year Resolutions* and *Wobblers*, but otherwise tends to obstruct the flow of most migratory cyclists.

Mamils and *Couriers* are known to hold *Office Magnets* in particular disdain, and think nothing of unseating one or two as they whizz past.

ADULT LEARNER

A most haphazard beast, the *Adult Learner* is all knees and elbows, pedals whizzing around on low gear even on the flat. Can be easily identified on a slope by the smell of burning breakpads, a curious scent that appears to do nothing at all for either prospective mates or other cyclists.

Commonly known as a general laughing stock amongst other breed of cyclist and most other fauna, the *Adult Learner* can often be encountered in parks and on pavements. Though a relatively silent beast (you can occasionally hear teeth grinding at busy intersections) the *Adult Learner's* passage is often accompanied by shouts of 'Oi!', 'Get back on the effin road!' and other expletives of that nature or worse.

The author has, indeed, heard one bedraggled creature receive no fewer than seven 'c**ts' on one small section of Glaswegian pavement.

Always bedecked with a oversized helmet, what sets this particular cyclist apart from other *Wobblers* is a set of hefty elbow and knee pads, either in black or in a lurid yellow.

On occasion an *Adult Learner* might be spotted in the countryside – a male, usually, who for reasons of mating display will mimic a *Tourer* (some sort of Cuckoo impulse, perhaps). This pathetic specimen will have a tight fluorescent plumage, and is often found, with feet clipped into pedals and face buried in the verge – probably searching for insects.

Habitat – Closely bound to the city
Range – Very limited, usually no further than the park gates
Voice – The grinding of teeth
Comfortable around – Disdained even by other Wobblers. Invariably terrorised by BMX Bandits.

ECO WARRIOR

This breed is resurgent after shifting political winds back in the naughties caused them to decline. With a warming climate, however, their numbers are booming, which is great news for spotters.

The *Eco Warrior* is a shaggy creature, though that should not be the only method used to identify them. The females of the species often have long dreadlocked hair and their thin-wheeled bicycles sport prominent wicker baskets. The males, on the other hand, sport handsome beards, the females often judging their potential mate's 'eco-credentials' by the size of said face fungus. Mature Eco-warriors are recognizable by a sizable appendage, known as a 'pull-along' or 'trolley', which extends out backwards and is used for carrying vegetables, allotment tools, or a small, grubby fledgling in a smock.

Colour variations differ greatly between individuals, and there are both crested and bareheaded subspecies, so these markings should not be used when it comes to identification. If visual markers are required, I recommend looking out for astonishing arrays of badges pinned to the plumage. An easier method of identification are mannerisms and psychology, as in this *Eco Warriors* stand out from all cyclists.

When travelling by road from roost to feeding ground (usually a smallholding) the *Eco Warrior* chooses where possible to ignore cars completely, and instead pretend that every road is a verdant country lane. Even in situations where communication is unavoidable – after a gentle collision at a road junction, for instance – the *Eco Warrior* looks at the driver with pity, or if it is a more confident older male, with utter disgust, before moving on with a damning shake of the head. This is in fact a defence mechanism, invoked by the fear of being crushed beneath a large carbon footprint.

Habitat – In ever increasing numbers in the city, though older members of the species often have large roosts in the countryside, known as 'communes'. Their presence often comes at the vanguard of rising house prices.

Range – Usually to be seen travelling between green areas, though at no great distance. Will travel further afield in pursuit of folk music, artisan bread, real ale and meals made from road-kill.

Voice – An annoyingly cheerful whistle, quoting statistics about ice melts and a repetitive warble of 'Hugh Fearnley-Wittingstall says...'

Comfortable around – Eco Warrior is comfortable around most species of cyclist, though encounters with an Electric Spirit often result in hurt looks and lectures on how electricity comes from carbon sources too, you know.

COUPLE'S COMPANION

T he *Couple's Companion* is a fascinating breed, and one that is still puzzling Cyclothologists today, after nearly a century of research. The two members of the species travel around together on the same two wheels, the dominant partner (or windbreaker) always in front. There have been no sightings as yet of a single member of this species travelling independently. This behavior requires high degrees of cooperation and an absence of a sense of smell from the rear partner.

Couple's Companions are very rare, a Giant Panda of cyclists. As such it is much sought after by spotters. The subspecies where both parties sport identical plumage are especially prized.

Couple's Companion is never seen in a city, unless it has been through serious error in navigation (there is one example on the internet of a pair trying to turn round in a narrow street in Leicester, with hilarious results). It is most likely to be spotted in the Fens, where the flat, straight roads are highly attractive. Occasional sightings are made at congregation points for a variety of breeds known as 'Centre Parcs', although these are always fleeting before a vicious fight breaks out between companions and the bicycle ends up in a ditch.

In his book *The Migratory Routes of Tourers, Across Europe and Beyond*, written just after the war by Captain PTSD Psychosis, it's mentioned that vast herds of these creatures can be found in the Black Forest of Germany. But as spotters may be aware, having been caught *in flagrante* with a female *Tipsey-Turvey* and following a highly publicized plagiarism scandal, Captain Psychosis's work is largely discredited.

Habitat – Flat, open countryside that has been well mapped and has straight roads.
Range – Usually they only make it five minutes from their roosts before fighting breaks out.
Voice – Squabbling, usually complaints by the lead partner that the other isn't pedaling hard enough.
Comfortable around – the other Sports (Novelties, Chaps, Flat Outs and Retro Perfectionists, who know what it is to be laughed at).

"Cyclists of the world unite; you have nothing to lose but your chains."

Karl Marx

ELECTRIC SPIRIT

There has been much debate in recent years as to whether or not *Electric Spirits* count as true cyclists, or whether they are in fact a separate genus entirely, but I have included them here because I find in their dogged spirits admirable.

These delightful little cyclists don't seem like much, but have a cunning trick up their sleeve; when a steep incline is approached they use an electric battery cunningly stored about their person to whizz up it without the need for strenuous pedaling. This can be no bad thing, as most *Electric Spirits* have wheels similar in size to the *Office Magnet* (this could, of course be a result of the electrification). My fellow COCK, Major Demented Elbow-Biter, suggested that the *Electric Spirit* may be the result of an unholy coupling between an *Office Magnet* and a motorcyclist, but this kind of genetic tinkering is an abomination and not to be encouraged.

The average *Electric Spirit* will have a bright, cheerful crest to match its bright, cheerful face, no doubt a result of the comfort and ease of its passage. Waterproof coats are another useful marker, though there has been an alarming rise in numbers of a puffer-jacketed subspecies, which is hopefully not another case of the bloat which has so blighted the *Oldie*.

Habitat – Few sightings in rural areas, or in northern cities.
Range – As far as the battery will allow. Has often been seen in roadside cafes waving a charger in hope.
Voice – Common cry of, 'Oh, isn't this such fun!' or 'Wheeee!'
Comfortable around – Hated by most cyclists for what is seen as 'cheating', though tolerated by the stronger species. *Gadgetman* is known to have a grudging respect for *Electric Spirit's* ingenuity.

BMX BANDIT

Also known as the *Terror*, the *BMX Bandit* is difficult to spot, as it is aggressively protective of territory. To prevent conflict with other cyclists, special reserves in parks have now been created.

Characterised by a thinning of plumage about the rear (also known as 'mooning') and a ridiculously low seat, *BMX Bandits* are rarely seen wearing crests, preferring instead a wide peak or cowl.

Never seen in any adult form, it has recently been discovered that *BMX Bandits* are in fact a prepubescent phase of the *Trickster* or *Mountain Ranger.* The juvenile *Bandit* is usually observed in a flock, or 'posse', performing gravity defying displays of superiority. The sight of so many cyclists jumping, hopping and spinning is impressive. As they develop their swooping and climbing skills fledgling *BMX Bandits* can be seen undergoing the initiation known as 'eating pavement'. If they cry, fledglings are rejected and cast out of the posse, sometimes for days on end.

Interestingly, the female *BMX Bandit*, also known as 'jail-bait', has no cycle and instead sits in a hoodie on the edges of the reserve chewing gum and sporting a look of utter boredom. Occasionally, late at night, they will lean against the handle bars of a male, and no more than once a year will accept the offer of a 'backie'. This intermittent sexual behavior often causes inter-species breeding between frustrated male BMXs and female *Skaters* which results in an ugly, misbegotten hybrid known as an *Emo.*

Avoid taking photos of the *BMX Bandit* on a smartphone as they will take it from you in the same way a Baboon will steal your hub caps.

Habitat – Confined exclusively to cities.
Range – Usually to the nearest park reserve, occasionally grouping outside fast food outlets in large groups known as 'grunts'.

Voice – An unintelligible language impossible to understand by spotters or other cyclists.

Comfortable around – *Tricksters*, where there is a strong sense of respect. They will happily share their reserve with a *Trickster* in exchange for a visual display. Will terrorise *Adult Learners* with jeers and taunts, and absolutely despise *Hipsters*.

NEW YEAR
RESOLUTION

The best time to see *New Year Resolutions* is, as the name suggests, in the first couple of weeks of January when they emerge in vast numbers that dwindle quickly. They are almost impossible to find by the first days of February. Where they spend the rest of the year is a mystery, but it is likely the *New Year Resolution* hibernates on soft sofas and dusty nooks through Spring, Summer, Autumn and Winter, gorging on fatty foods on the rare occasions it emerges.

A graceless creature, this cyclist can be found lumbering around in most towns and villages, sweating profusely. An ancient folk tale suggests the *New Year Resolution* not only heralds the start of the year, but actually instigates Spring, due to the huge volumes of water and heat generated. Long recognised as fable, the idea still holds strength in some inbred parts of Norfolk.

Often clad in an ill-fitting crest several sizes too small, and grey baggy 'sweat plumage', it is often best to look for the small cloud of superheated air around the cranium when identifying, though the sight of such a large, overweight body enveloping a creaking, poorly maintained bicycle, is hard to miss and impossible to mistake for any other breed.

Habitat – All built-up conurbations, from hamlets to cities.
Range – Often small circles around the roost, though some adventurous urban members will also make their way to feeding grounds in city centres.
Voice – Heavy wheezing.
Comfortable around – The *New Year Resolution* is around for such a short time that it is hard to gauge their affinity with other cycling types. Usually obstruct *Mamils*, leading to friction.

TIPSY-TURVEY

To spot this cyclist, you really need to be out and about in the wee small hours – between 2 and 3am is best – although there is always a chance of one being spotted during daylight if it hasn't been locked up for its own safety.

Tipsy-Turveys have two speeds; very slow or perilously fast. When in the slow mode they creep along, head and neck as low as the handlebars, face taut with concentration, eyes fixated on a point thirty centimetres ahead of the front wheel. When in fast mode the extreme posture is even more pronounced, the chin touching the handlebars and gaze welded to the front wheel, mesmerized by the spinning tyres.

If the spotter requires any further methods of verification, the following can be used: the eyes of a *Tipsy-Turvey* are always half closed, often with a watery glaze, and the skin will have a grave, sweat-covered pallor. A crude, unlit cigarette will be stuck to the bottom lip, and the cyclist will periodically stop, attempt to light said cigarette, fail and start moving again.

Spending the day at feeding grounds in public houses, they are only seen returning to roost – it is thought that in the afternoon they return for another liquid supper using some sort of camouflage that makes it easy to mistake them for ordinary cyclists.

Habitat – Anywhere a drinking establishment is present. A marked decline in village pubs has hit the rural population hard, although they occasionally emerge from home-based sessions to forage for 'scran'.

Range – Between roost and watering hole, preferably within two miles.

Voice – Slurred speech, occasionally breaking into snatches of unintelligible songs.

Comfortable around – Due to their preferred nocturnal existence *Tipsy-Turveys* are never seen near any breed of cyclist, save the occasional grunt of *BMX Bandits*, which is ignored like everything else.

MAMIL

T he *Mamil* is probably the fastest-growing breed of cyclist today. Almost exclusively male, these silver foxes are often adorned in a brightly coloured plumage, worn very close to the skin. As with other breeds of *Sprinter* it sports the ingenious pouch fixed to its back, where sundry handy objects can be secreted without spilling when entering the pouncing position.

It is thought that, with their pouncing posture (bum up, head down, back straight, arms tight by the side, gripping the fearsome hooked handlebars) and rapid speeds, these cyclists were once predators. It may be that the thrill of the chase proved more exciting than that of the catch. Nowadays *Mamils* are more interested in carb-loading than being carnivores.

The shape of the *Mamil* is one that has been honed by the wind; they are lithe, long and lean, expanding only around the paunch, which sits in a natural lee. Their crests are long tear shapes in plain white or black. Many *Mamils* enjoy sporting a large bulge below the paunch, for display purposes. This can be accentuated by purchasing trousers two sizes too small. *Mamils* with particularly small bulges are met with derision by others of the breed.

Habitat – Born to ride, they can be found cycling their stuff all over the United Kingdom.
Range – Never keen to spend nights away from home, the Mamil will always be home before dark to prevent 'getting grief'.
Voice – Annoying boasting about how healthy they feel nowadays.
Comfortable around – The *Mamil* is keen to chat to other *Sprinters*, especially the *Tourer*, but cannot stand those who are not fully embracing the Lycra dream, especially the *Fairweather Wanderer*.

SHERIFF

T he *Sheriff* is the king of the road, and isn't afraid to prove it. A rare cyclist, he has taken it upon himself to be expert on current legislation regarding treatment of cyclists in the wild, and is determined to enforce the law rigorously. You will hear him before you see him, as he upbraids taxis, pedestrians, other cars and especially buses for minor infringements of the *Highway Code*. When he gets onto the legality of not wearing a helmet it becomes a spectator sport.

Distinguished by actions rather than looks, a *Sheriff* is best identified by his flinty, eagle-eyed, eternally vigilant facial expression. He often rears up like a meerkat, standing up on his pedals, to scan the perimeter for miscreants to accost. Members of the breed have even been seen with a small head-mounted wing mirror, which had always been regarded as sole preserve of *Gadgetman*.

The *Sheriff's* badge is a video camera. These are attached to the helmet, and often point backwards, to catch bus drivers as they encroach on the *Sheriff's* substantial personal space.

Habitat – Solely urban, preferring the busiest commuter highways where the most traffic violations occur.

Range – Tend to stick to their individual commutes, from roost to feeding ground, but always leave an extra hour each way for disciplinary measures.

Voice – Loud and strident, occasionally shrill, will put listeners in a bad mood for the rest of the day.

Comfortable around – All cyclists are in fear of the *Sheriff*, and try to stay out of sight as much as possible.

TOURER

T he *Tourer* is the wildebeest of cyclists, travelling in long migrations all year round, regardless of weather or road conditions. *Tourers* range the mountain passes of Scotland and the long spines of the Pennines. In the sixties it was not unusual to see whole herds disembark from specially adapted trains before setting off together into the last wild places.

Sadly, this is no longer the case. The rapid growth in numbers of *Juggernauts* (see *Predators*, p.106) in recent decades has lead to the disappearance of larger herds, the *Tourer* becoming solitary, never to be found in packs larger than three or four individuals. Having said that, vast numbers of *Tourers* will congregate at watering holes in remote areas to compare war stories as they drink protein shakes and feast exclusively on bananas. Although similar to the *Mamil* in terms of plumage, the *Tourer* has the grace and elegance to look like he was born in Lycra. They are invariably softly spoken, earnest creatures, belying the wealth of experience that other cyclists can't touch. Some *Tourers* have been known to utilise the 'thousand yard stare' defence behaviour against other breeds seeking to gain cool points by talking to them. *Tourers* are known to interbreed with European examples they meet in windswept places, but since they never nest, no hybrid progeny have ever been spotted.

Habitat – The open road. Houses are an anathema to them, cities doubly so.
Range – The length and breadth of the country, and beyond if they can find passage to Europe.
Voice – Soft and measured, echoing with the memory of a thousand miles with nothing but the wind for company.
Comfortable around – Only other *Tourers*. No other cyclist has anything to offer.

GADGETMAN

T his is the Swiss Army Knife of cyclists, an obsessive collector of tools, widgets and gizmos. Since the moment that cyclists were discovered there have been *Gadgetmen*, wielding a frankly unmanageable number of tricks and toys.

Their bikes are covered in little devices that measure everything imaginable, from windspeed to distance travelled to saddle friction. The only thing they don't have a clue about it how to look after their steed, and they will often be seen attempting to change a tyre at the side of the road with little success.

Gadgetman loves to talk. You will often find one sitting outside to a watering hole with their bicycle, talking to anyone within earshot about 'this great new device you can clip on your collar and it tells you when you're breathing too hard'.

When actually riding their mounts, *Gadgetmen* travel slowly due to the sheer weight of equipment attached. However, at least they know exactly how slowly they are going, to the nearest foot per second. *Gadgetman* is a COCKS officially endangered breed as, to quote the citation, they can 'never get laid'. No such thing as a *Gadgetwoman* exists and other breeds fall instantly asleep as soon as they get within in touching distance.

Habitat – Both urban and rural, but due to the weight of gadgetry avoids hilly areas.
Range – According to their cyclometer, they've managed 1500 miles this month! Pretty cool, huh?
Voice – High-pitched nasal twang, extremely repetitive call.
Comfortable around – *Mamils* are the only cyclists that will put up with the *Gadgetman*, because they find them genuinely interesting. Some believe that *Gadgetmen* are actually not a stand-alone breed in their own right but are merely *Mamils* with no mates.

FAMILY TREE

T he *Family Tree* bears close resemblance to the toddler toy that comprises of a large duck on a piece of string, to which three or four ducklings are attached. Some quirk of evolution has given members of this breed the ability to retain the umbilical cord. The dominant parent attaches the siblings before travel and has a curious repetitive twitch, constantly looking over its shoulder every 5 seconds regardless of location. At least one fledgling is crying at any one time. With no obvious source of food (the dominant parent having forgotten to bring the packed lunches) the other fledglings feed off their own bogies to survive.

The unattached, submissive parent stays separate from the group, and instead circles about the *Tree*, making sure they are clear of danger whilst muttering passive-aggressive criticisms of the dominant parent under its breath. Though in some respects they share similar characteristics with the *Eco Warrior*, the *Family Tree* does not have the same laid-back approach, instead remaining hysterical with fear at all times.

Habitat – Busy high streets and parks, especially in summer when everyone else is outside.

Range – As long as the route is smooth, it is astonishing how many dangerous situations a Family Tree can find itself in.

Voice – Incessant groans from the beast of burden, whilst the guardian cyclist omits regular shrieks.

Comfortable around – The *Lesser Spotted Wobbler* and the *Oldie*, simply because they tend to be in even more trouble and thus act as a perfect shield from predators.

SIT-UP-AND-BEG

T hese striking creatures have a grace that belies their frame of steel, which makes them formidable if coming at you in a stampede. To avoid this, keep away from newly-launched delicatessens, allotment open days, and anywhere that does a healthy brunch after twelve on a Sunday.

They have an interesting history, having not been seen in the UK until the forties, when a breeding pair were taken from Germany and brought here as spoils of war. Since then they have proliferated, and are now found in most cities, but in very high concentration around posh universities.

The favourite pastime of the average *Sit-Up-And-Beg* is to whimsically float about leafy streets with baskets full of delicacies, laughing gaily and enjoying the summer sun. They are rarely seen in winter, when their weight counts against them in wet and icy conditions. *Sit-Up-And-Begs* never undertake cycle maintenance of any kind, because 'Daddy always sorts it out'.

Dressed in flowing summer dresses or rolled-up trousers and tiny T-shirts, they are highly picturesque and as a result appear in many corporate photoshoots and TV adverts. They of course love the attention. The *Sit-Up-And-Beg's* principal defensive strategy is distraction. *Mamils* are particularly susceptible to disappearing under the wheels of a *Juggernaut* having first been hypnotized by a passing example.

Habitat – Verdant glades and fairy grottos, streets around academic institutions offering degrees in Art, Italian or English Literature.

Range – What is distance when you have long summer evenings and lashings of home brewed elderflower champagne?

Voice – Merry laughter and tinkling of bells.

Comfortable around – Hipsters, Couriers (when going through its 'bit-of-rough' phase) and to a lesser degree *Novelties* (nothing so funny as a *Novelty*, tee-hee). Detests *Metal Stallions*, because no-body likes to be reminded of jobs and work.

METAL STALLION

T he workhorse of the cyclist genus, *Metal Stallions* are dull and efficient. Not for them carbon fibre frames or low-profile tyres, but instead a functional mountain bike with worn tyres and simple fluorescent chest feathers that get the job done.

Very occasionally you may come across a sub-breed that has evolved a saddle bag, wherein additional subdued, functional work plumage resides (it will be charcoal grey and white or light blue) for arrival at the feeding grounds where there is never any funny business. On Fridays, when headed for the watering hole, the saddle bag may include a blouson leather jacket.

On the pitted commuter roads *Metal Stallions* can be seen both morning and evening, head down, legs churning, just wanting to get the work done with the minimum of fuss.

One of my earliest spotting memories is standing with my father at a junction on a frosty January morning in Manchester and, as the lights turned red, watching four or five of these noble creatures come to a halt within touching distance. I will never forget hearing their great lungs suck in air, seeing the clouds of steam escaping their nostrils like bulls.

While remarkably robust in most environments, *Metal Stallions* die in large numbers each year when their identity cards, displayed on lanyards around their necks, get snagged on passing wing mirrors.

Habitat – The cold, sterile environment of an open plan office. Always with booths.

Range – Distance doesn't matter, as long as there are no deviations from the route.

Voice – Atonal, brusque, never offers two calls where one will do.

Comfortable around – Simply ignores most frivolous breed of cyclist, especially *Wobblers*. Has a grudging respect for *Gadgetman* for his expertise and *Courier* for his efficiency.

RACER

Outrageously competitive, *Racers* get a thrill from beating you even when you are standing still. They are aloof, unwilling to engage in any form of interaction outside competition.

Fastidious in their plumage, when not racing they will spend hours preening; making sure their shorts are just the right degree of tight, that their jerseys are spotless (unless they are spotty), and that their undercarriage is tuned to perfection.

But beneath that snobbish exterior is a masochistic heart, *Racers* able to punish themselves twice as hard as they ever punish their rivals. One example is in their constant battle with body hair. A *Racer's* legs will be as smooth as a trunk of bamboo, and just as tough.

Retired *Racers* often join the rag trade. Unlike other breeds, *Racers* love needles.

Habitat – There is nowhere they won't go for a chance to give another cyclist a thrashing.

Range – Distance is immaterial: winning is everything.

Voice – Stony silence is all you will be faced with.

Comfortable around – Incompatible with most other cyclists, who just aren't interested in that level of competition. Has been known to hang about with *Couriers*, but gets frustrated with their supercool nonchalance.

MOUNTAIN RANGER

T he *Mountain Ranger* is happiest off-road, thundering down muddy trails, flying over piles of rocks and logs. In fact, the *Mountain Ranger* spends so much time trying to fly, early spotters thought it'd evolved from a primitive, ugly bird.

Though it shouldn't be hard to mistake due to the terrain you find it in, another failsafe method for spotting is to look at the *Mountain Ranger's* crest, which has a pronounced brim or visor and often a hard transparent coating (also known as 'goggles') over its wild, staring eyes. Often it will also have a perforated cover across its face so that, when it lets out an adrenalin-induced scream, insects, mud, twigs and rabbit droppings don't disappear down its gaping maw.

Also recognisable at rest by its flattened nose and dented pate, the *Mountain Ranger* is notably lacking in any manner of self-preservation or common sense. Throwing himself down the steepest of inclines for no apparent gain, it has also been suggested that he's in fact a *Metal Stallion* whose girlfriend has just dumped him. More likely is that the *Mountain Ranger* is in fact a *BMX Bandit* who has grown bored of masturbation. As such they are not the most numerous of breeds, principally because foresters and landowners regard them as vermin who destroy the environment and who should be shot on sight. They are also vilified for habits similar to beavers, creating huge complex structures out of logs in the middle of forests. The COCKS environmental lobby argues that, like pigs rooting for truffles, *Mountain Rangers* turn over upland soil aiding aeration and plant growth and therefore deserve thanks and respect. Sadly this is invariably met with howls of derision.

Habitat – Mountains, ravines, anywhere you might feel your heart in your mouth.
Range – From very high up to very far down.

Voice – Wild whooping, many expletives.

Comfortable around – Though not terribly sociable, they do hold some affinity with *BMX Bandits*.

"Shadow is the means by which cyclists display their form."

Leonardo Da Vinci

HIPSTER

A poseur amongst cyclists, the *Hipster* (also known as the *Marsh Bed-wetter*) is a byword for style with little substance. They wear ill-fitting tweed, cycling caps in lurid colours, and their leg plumage will always stop above the ankle, allowing full sight of brightly-coloured stripey socks and fancy designer shoes, which invariably have soles that match the tread on their bicycle's tyres. Around the *Hipster's* waist is a large bicycle chain, slung low so that a vintage belt can still be seen clearly. *Hipsters* are never seen without geeky glasses, nor an ironic, superior smirk on their winsome faces.

Hipsters are the cuckoos of the cyclist world, as when they start to infest an area you can be sure most other species will vanish quickly. Rising cost of roosts and a proliferation of retro shops make other breeds too nauseated to bear staying.

Hipsters thrive off being seen, and should be an easy first catch for a new spotter. A word of warning, however; don't go for a refreshment in any area where large concentrations of *Hipsters* gather, as you will be bamboozled by the vast range of free-trade coffees, herbals infusions and craft beers on offer.

It has been claimed that most *Hipsters* die when their floppy fringes cause them to crash. However this is impossible to verify as fellow *Hipsters* invariably recycle every part of any carcass.

Habitat – The trendiest places in town, in parks, outside crowd-funded cafés and artisan bakeries.
Range – Never strays far from a Wholefoods or organic vegetable co-operative.
Voice – An irritating crowing, holding forth on obscure Art House films and the Pitchfork 100.
Comfortable around – Only other *Hipsters*, and mirrors.

THE COURIER

L ike a *Mamil* but without the penchant for Lycra, *Couriers* are the business end of cycling. They are everything that *Hipsters* aspire to be, but without the tweeness. Less mature *Hipsters* can occasionally be mistaken for *Couriers* due to both breeds' penchant for army surplus, particularly forage caps. The clearest signpost for spotters is a large bag or pouch strapped from shoulder to hip, or occasionally larger packages and boxes are tied on their backs. Even with this weight they go at speeds that would put *Mamils* to shame.

Couriers need high levels of adrenalin to survive, due to their highly dangerous habitat (see *Predators* for examples). As such, they often congregate in groups to share acts of derring-do as part of their mating rituals. It is not uncommon to see them racing on ice-covered canals, or through building sites, as tests of virility.

Best observed out-of-doors in full flight. When spied in office receptions chatting up the office manager, *Couriers* can appear, in the harsh interior light, as grubby and badly groomed.

For yet unexplained reasons *Couriers* always disappear on Friday afternoons. Legend has it they go to a secret place known only to themselves to enact a ritual referred to as the 'toke'.

Habitat – Usually dense urban areas with lots of businesses. Rarely seen in residential nesting grounds.
Range – Will travel only as far as their radios can pick up a signal.
Voice – Can be heard over the noise of traffic, yelling abuse at pedestrians and drivers who encroach on their route.
Comfortable around – At their best when around their own kind, as all other cyclists are 'fucking amateurs', but they have a grudging respect for *Mountain Rangers*. Often followed around by bunches of proto-hipsters, who they loathe. Love bating *Sheriffs* by jumping red lights, cycling on pavements and through busy pedestrian precincts while not holding the handlebars.

Robbie Guillory

LESSER-SPOTTED
WOBBLER

J ust as some Brown Trout become Sea Trout, occasionally an *Adult Learner* will fall off the pavement and become a *Lesser-Spotted Wobbler*. These are nervous cyclists, more or less paralyzed with fear, who have virtually no control over their mounts. Many comparisons have been made between *Lesser-Spotted Wobblers* and fainting goats, as both fall over when surprised.

To photograph these cyclists in action you must use a hide or camouflage. If they see you they will either be unable to get their feet in the right place for pedaling or will just tumble over with fright. When coming face to face with a predator, some may even involuntarily defecate – a kind of extreme defensive response.

It is very difficult to observe a *Lesser-Spotted Wobbler* on any form of migration, as they often never get more than a few metres from their roosts before deciding to go home, have a cup of tea and try again tomorrow. Some have suggested they are in fact the only flightless breed of cyclist. However the *Lesser-Spotted Wobbler's* only saving grace is that, once it actually hits the road, there are so many things to terrify it, it doesn't actually know which way to fall, which is where the wild wobbling motion originates.

Habitat – Very close to their houses, but also congregate outside hospitals.
Range – The outside world is too scary to get far.
Voice – Shrill screaming, gastric rumblings.
Comfortable around – Only truly comfortable when in the roost.

THE NOVELTY

N ot to be confused with *Flat Outs, Novelties* are cyclists who have dismissed the conventional mount in favour of the unicycle or other cycles that have evolved in bizarre ways.

These unusual creatures were, until recently, considered 'sports' – not worthy of classification and best ignored or, better still, eradicated, but after a YouTube video of a tiny *Novelty* on a Penny Farthing went viral they have become the focus of massive public interest.

Spotters are reminded that while filming *Novelties* can be a good way of offsetting the costs associated with our chosen hobby, it is unethical to force or intimidate this gentle breed into pulling a funny face, saying the F-word or other deliberate attempts at cuteness. Anyone seen to do so will be prosecuted by COCKS and risks having his or her membership revoked.

Habitat – parks, precincts, festivals and anywhere with a camera phone and internet connection.
Range – They never get far, the poor misguided creatures.
Voice – Imbecilic giggling.
Comfortable around – They get very shy around other cyclists, but have a liking for the similarly ridiculous *Flat Outs* and *Chaps*.

BERSERKER

N amed after Norse warriors, this species of cyclist is terrifying to behold, a whirlwind of spitting, gnashing, fist-waving fury that is feared by pedestrians, other cyclists and motorists alike.

Road rage is a permanent mental state for the *Berserker*. No flight for them, just fight. This can be an advantage as all that built-up rage means they have extraordinary acceleration and charging speed. Spotters will recognise them as they hurtle through everything from police cordons to red lights, furiously yelling at anyone or thing that gets in their way.

Linguists suggest that *Berserkers* are the source of all new swearwords that enter the lexicon. *Beserkers* are least likely to say 'No, after you...' Most likely to say, 'You f***ing f**k!! Get out of my f***ing way!!'

Safe to say, never taunt a *Beserker*. Whatever you do, don't ask if they were bottle-fed as a baby. They're likely to bite you. Best to lie down and play possum. When they don't get a reaction they'll go find someone else to pick a fight with.

Habitat – Built for the fjords, but found amongst Fords.
Range – They can go and go until the anger runs out. Which is never.
Voice – A guttural growl, near unintelligible, or a primal scream.
Comfortable around – Surprisingly, *Berserkers* and *Sheriffs* get on like a house on fire, sharing as they do an absolute disdain for all other life-forms.

TRICKSTER

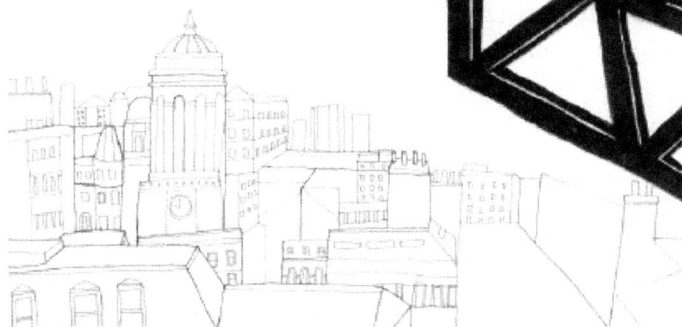

Robbie Guillory

T he *Trickster* is an adult *BMX Bandit* who could never get a girlfriend and is caught in an endless vortex of trying to impress a non-existent audience, gaining some sense of meaning through constantly posting videos on social media. All of the *Trickster's* friends have got married and become accountants (though some have evolved into *Mountain Rangers*) and the *Trickster* is often seen with a gaggle of fledgling BMX Bandits around him like some latter-day Fagan.

When dismounted the *Trickster* can be mistaken for non-cyclist species such as *Trendy Dad* and the fearsome *Football Casual*, such is their penchant for hoodies, grey stubble, Beats and Stone Island. Plumage is often as bare at the rear as a *BMX Bandit* but the *Trickster* is not the terror it once was. Instead, that pack-induced aggression has been turned inward, transforming into an iron determination to get mortally injured in as many ways as possible.

This compulsion lures *Tricksters* away from the safe confines of the skate park to try their luck on the hard, sharp edges and spikes of the real world. The internet is full of these lithe, muscular beasts on their tiny bikes, jumping off ledges onto railings, and spinning from there to hop down stairs before falling and having ten teeth knocked out. Some spotters collect teeth and body parts shed by *Tricksters*, although I personally do not condone the practice.

Habitat – The urban jungle, preferably pedestrianised areas with plenty of street furniture.
Range – Though they ride for long periods of time, their routes are so convoluted that they never get far.
Voice – A repetitive call that sounds like 'Ouch!'
Comfortable around – *BMX Bandits*, and like *Novelties* because they make even the *Trickster* seem cool.

"The sexual life of adult cyclists is a 'dark continent' for cyclothologists"

Sigmund Freud

FLAT OUT

T he laziest of all cyclist species would have to be the *Flat Out*. So casual is their style of riding that they modify their bicycles to do it lying down, gazing languidly forward through their toes. John Lennon and Yoko Ono are believed to have been the first *Flat Outs* although no actual evidence of this survives.

These 'recumbents,' as they are also known, have the turning circle of a drunk cow, so in traffic *Flat Outs* often have the appearance of manatees swimming with dolphins. They always wear dark glasses, which only adds to the overall air of a cyclist on perennial holiday. All that is missing is the ice-cream.

Some Cyclothologists believe the horizontal posture is actually some form of sexual display, although no spotter has ever observed the *Flat Out* mating while still mounted.

Finding out where a *Flat Out* is can be relatively simple; the spotter has but to slowly scan the city for a cluster of people pointing and laughing – a sure sign that you will strike gold in their midst.

Habitat – Long, straight, flat roads, with gentle corners.
Range – Oh, not too far today. Or any day, for that matter.
Voice – A slow drawl, as if tomorrow is always there for when things need doing.
Comfortable around – Everyone.

THE RETRO
PERFECTIONIST

This is a beautiful cyclist to observe, but one that is in sad decline due to the nature of their recycled lifestyle. After all, their numbers are limited by the amount of authentic memorabilia out there to feed their obsession. Watching a small flock of these is like footage from a Pathé newsreel. *Retro Perfectionists* scour junkyards, car boot sales, eBay and thrift shops in search of old, classic steel-framed bicycles, leather helmets, mildewed saddles and any other paraphernalia of bygone days. All the better if they have to restore them first. In this they are the antithesis of the *Mamil* and a kind of weird mirror image of the *Gadgetman*.

Closely related to the *Hipster*, but more ascetic and less self-obsessed, these veterans can be identified with ease. Look for a small, peaked corduroy cap rather than helmet, a plumage of merino wool, a bow-tie and small leather feet. A well-tended handlebar moustache, waxed at the ends, is also an excellent marker of a *Retro Perfectionist*.

Pedalling wearing such heavy equipment has provided the *Retro Perfectionist* with one other identifying feature – their enormous appetite. They burn calories so fast as to require only the richest, sweetest, stickiest foodstuffs, particularly Cornish pasties and cream teas, in vast quantities. A few pints of ale from a heritage brewery never go amiss either!

Habitat – Country lanes, migration routes between architectural salvage yards, anywhere the Mamils think is challenging.
Range – To the ends of the earth, if there is a rusted pre-war handlebar bell at the end of it.
Voice – A loud, jolly account of saddle sores picked up at L'Eroica in Italy.
Comfortable around – Enjoys the company of *Tourers*, loves looking down on *Mamils* but find *Gadgetmen* strangely arousing. Also

enjoys bating other *Retro Perfectionists* about mounts that are not 100% authentic.

THE RAG AND BONE MAGPIE

T he flatbed truck of cyclists, the *Rag and Bone Magpie* cannot pass a pile of rubbish without stopping to look through it for useful bits and pieces. They ride mounts modified from the detritus of the streets into great flatbed tricycles, all the better to collect more junk! And what do they do with what they pick up? Make more tricycles of course.

It's isn't known why they do this, as there seems to be no end-purpose to these contraptions, although they may be members of some kind of survivalist sect that is convinced that a worldwide epidemic is about to wipe out manufacturing and they better get used to make-and-mend improvisation.

There was a Cyclothologist's theory that *Rag and Bone Magpies* are like hermit crabs, building bigger and bigger shells, moving from one vehicle to another. Further study of them in the wild revealed that they are fiercely protective of all they make, and can have up to fifty contraptions by the time they expire.

Spotters need little extra information to aid identification, but it may be of interest to them that the tools that *Rag and Bone Magpies* use are actually fashioned from the bicycles of their dead ancestors, and some may be many hundreds of years old.

Habitat – Urban areas with a large student population, for better pickings.
Range – Their contraptions are good for carrying things, but not for movement. Limited to a couple of miles.
Voice – 'There's no such thing as useless rubbish'
Comfortable around – Gadgetmen.

THE OLDIE

*O*ldies are elegant creatures. Their headcrests come in a selection of pastel shades, with tufts of blue-rinse sprouting from the base to warm their ears and necks. Both sexes sport a long flowing plumage with a handy waterproof coating, and large, useful pockets.

Their bicycles are generally similar to those driven by *Sit Up and Begs*, but due to the spine curvature experienced by *Oldies* you would be forgiven for thinking otherwise, as their chins are often closer to the handlebars than most *Mamils*.

When venturing out to observe the *Oldie*, spotters should take care – these creatures are notoriously short-sighted, and are liable to run you down without noticing. This can be difficult to avoid as the *Oldie* never moves in a straight line, but instead wobbles and weaves all over the road, quite oblivious to the panic, disorder and (often) destruction in their wake. A lesser-seen variant (pictured here) carries an aged hound in a wicker pouch sitting over the front wheel.

Habitat – Rarely ventures into heavily built-up areas or city centres. Often found in villages or suburbs.
Range – Just to the shops and back... if the *Oldie* can remember where back is.
Voice – A call of 'Oh, sorry dear, didn't see you lying there.'
Comfortable around – *Sit Up and Begs*, to whom they are often related, *Fairweathers* and *Sheriffs*.

FAIRWEATHERS

T rue to their name, you will never see a *Fairweather* on a rainy day. They only come out when conditions are just right – not too hot or windy, nor too cold or wet. Where they spend the rest of their year, and how they can survive without leaving their roosts for food and water, is a mystery. It has been suggested that they gather vast quantities of food when they are out and about and store them in hidden pouches like hamsters, but this seems doubtful.

The males have plumage that rarely goes below the knee or upper arms, and the chest will be white or a bright, primary colour pattern, whilst the females will float along in a light, flowing plumage of a light blue or pastel shade. They will be laughing, smiling brightly and discussing how glorious it is to be out on their bicycles. From this we infer that their dormant periods are dispiritingly boring.

In their baskets will be all the prerequisites for their mating courtship rituals: fizzy Italian wine, plastic glasses, a gingham tablecloth, a baguette, some soft cheeses and various cured meats. In the late sixties, the breed was threatened when penniless hippies took to ambushing mating pairs and making off with their picnics.

Habitat – Clearings in wooded glens, with a tinkling stream and the sun shining soft and green through the leaves, also quiet country roads and secluded bays at sunset. Before setting out they congregate at M&S, gathering provisions.
Range – Ten miles if the spot at the end is just right.
Voice – A variety of melodic calls from 'Oh, isn't this fun!' and 'Why don't we do this more often?' to 'What lovely weather!', 'A touch more fizz, Bubbles?' and 'Rather, thanks!'
Comfortable around – They are oblivious to all other cyclists.

THE CHAP

An eccentric, known to have a penchant for cups of tea and crumpets. The *Chap's* crest varies, but is often a Bowler, Trilby or Panama.

The great event for spotters is the annual rutting at Henley, where male *Chaps* from across the country gather to joust with umbrellas for the attentions of females.

Easy to spot in their dull plumage of greenish tweed above and red (or salmon) denim around the legs. *The Chap* is becoming steadily rarer in the British Isles; no doubt a result of the loss of the now extinct *Butler* – a breed which was only interested in the feeding and grooming of *Chaps* – and the steady decline of tea rooms which has so drastically reduced the supply of cucumber sandwiches the *Chap* relies on.

Recently London Zoo took a breeding pair of *Chaps* into captivity to see if there may be a way to reverse their fortunes. So far they have mostly occupied themselves with playing bicycle croquet, drinking claret and checking their portfolio in the FT, but the keepers are hopeful that this may be a protracted mating ritual.

Habitat – The winding paths of country estates, cobbled mews of Bloomsbury and various literary festivals including Cheltenham and Hay.

Range – Is willing to travel many miles for a 'decent bloody gin and tonic'.

Voice – The hailing cry of 'What Ho!' is well known, and is often followed by a guttural gurgle of 'Jollygoodjollygoodjollygood'. Also known to quote Pliny in the original Latin.

Comfortable around – *Chaps* are known to be comfortable patronising all types of cyclist, but they are rarely seen with any but their own kind. Collectively known as a 'garden party'.

THIEVING BASTARD

T *hieving Bastards* are the great unknown, and I have only included them because, on the balance of things, they must exist. These are the true parasites of the species, cannibals, scavengers, creatures so cunning as to be able to, chameleon-like, display like any cyclist they choose, based on habitat and mount left unattended.

The only evidence we do have for their existence are the grieving cyclists found bereft of their bicycles, weeping bitter tears onto the battered remnants of their chains and locks.

There is no way to know how the *Thieving Bastard* came to be so nefarious, but other cyclists hate them with a passion, and often gather together in packs, known as a 'Critical Mass', to hunt them down with pitchforks and burning torches.

One theory is that *Thieving Bastards* are employed by *Rag and Bone Magpies* who live in particularly clean areas. Various religious rituals have been used over the years in an attempt to thwart them, including the 'invisible marker', but all have proved ineffectual.

Habitat – Everywhere and nowhere, in the shadows, in plain sight. It could be behind you right now.
Range – Unknown, but judging by bicycle thefts, very wide.
Voice – Silent as the night.
Comfortable around – No one. Other cyclists will kill on sight.

SPORTSMAN

T he *Sportsman* (or *Sportswoman*, as the female of the species is known) is irritating and universally derided by other cyclists. Both sexes have white plumage, known as 'sweats', occasionally with a colour trim for decoration. Their bicycle or torso is adorned with a large sac, in which they keep a variety of racquets, balls and towels. These bulbous protrusions seem to have evolved in order to deliberately obscure the vision of other breeds competing with the *Sportsman* on Britain's roads.

Other than that, the contents of the sacs are only used to hit balls at each other. Occasionally, in the suburbs, an avid spotter might see a fledgling *Sportsman* carrying an oversized bag with metal clubs rattling about inside. These 'mini-golfers' are particularly unstable, likely to swerve in front of a passing vehicle at any moment, but shouldn't be mistaken for a *Lesser Spotted Wobbler.*

There is one activity that *Sportsmen* engage in that is worthwhile observing, 'bicycle polo'. When the moon is full, down alleys and in multistorey car parks, twenty or so cyclists will gather. They split into two groups, and then use a mallet or racquet to propel a small ball past the opposing team into a 'goal'. During such a match (possibly a form of mating ritual?) the degree of bicycle control is breathtaking. Be sure, however, to leave before the end of a match. After that comes the 'crowing', where winning *Sportsmen* boast loudly about their prowess, boring all those present to tears.

Habitat – Urban areas containing rectangular areas of closely cut grass.
Range – For a good match, they have been known to travel to different cities.
Voice – Repetitive call, 'Best out of three?'
Comfortable around – admire *Mamils* and *Tourers* for their com-

petitiveness.

RUSTBUCKET

I f Sloth was manifest on a bicycle, it would be the *Rustbucket*. This breed takes no care of its precious steeds, and is content instead to rattle along with the sure knowledge that if something does break, it will probably be fixable with a length of string.

Rustbuckets are believed to be closely related to *Hipsters*, and could possibly be the evolutionary link between them and the now sadly extinct *Hippy*. As such, the plumage of a *Rustbucket* will be close to that of a *Hipster*, though not nearly as well-groomed. They favour thin, brightly coloured plumage with bare arms and, rather than carefully selecting this from hyper-cool vintage shops, they tend to scavenge at jumble sales and have been known to break into textile banks outside shopping centres.

Retro Perfectionists are known to get very excited on the approach of a *Rustbucket* until they realise that the steed being used is just a battered Ridgeback rather than an original 40s Raleigh.

Habitat – They roost in the cooler but cheaper parts of University towns and cities. Congregate annually in Bristol for the *Rustbucket* mating season.

Range – Just to the shops, avoiding any cobbles lest bits fall off.

Voice – A metallic clatter followed by a blithe, 'Was that something important?'

Comfortable around – Get on well with *Hipsters*, hated by *Sheriffs*, as they give cyclists a 'bad name'.

HIRED OUT

Y ou may come across a *Hired Out* in your travels. This is not a breed of cyclist, though you would be forgiven for thinking it was one. Rather, what you are observing is part of a new phenomenon, mimic behavior caused by a virulent airborne infection that creates a form of homage or re-enactment in another species. Individuals dress up as a cyclist in order to ride around on a specially adapted, time-limited mount for a while.

Research by COCKS suggests the disease was brought to this country by a notorious carrier known only as 'Boris'.

Hired Outs are becoming ever more visible, and you will currently see them in at least four major cities in the UK. There isn't a good way to tell if the cyclist you are watching is an impersonator, as some of them have become extremely good at mimicking their favourite species (*Wobblers* are extremely popular, as are *Office Magnets*), but a good pointer is any writing or obvious branding on the bicycles – these will have been rented from a bicycle farmer rather than grown organically, and as such will be clearly marked.

Another way to unmask a *Hired Out* imposter is to see how other cyclists react. *Hired Outs* long for acceptance within herds of wild cyclists, but though sometimes their skills are deft, they smell strange, and as such are avoided like the plague by true pedigree breeds.

THE CUCKOO

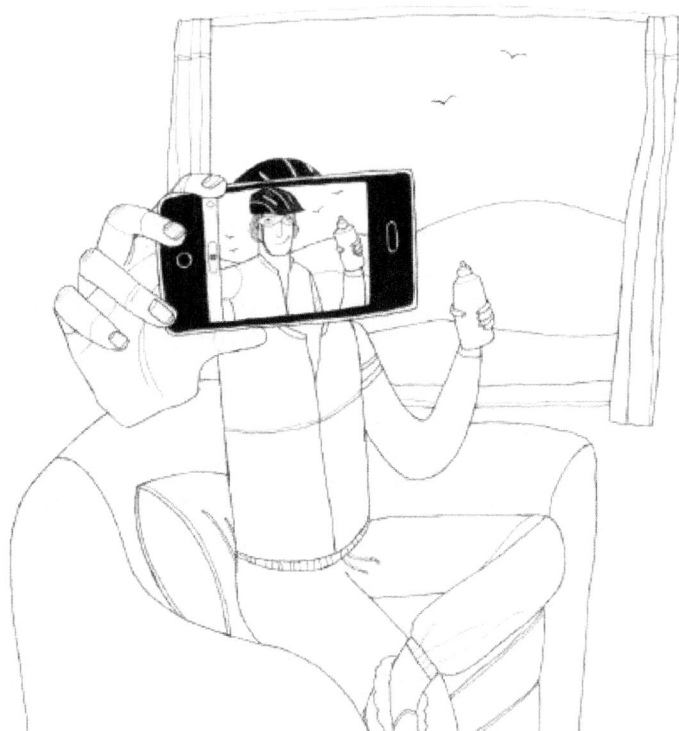

Another faux-cyclist, the *Cuckoo* is a strange individual who has a desire to act like a cyclist; to dress up in false plumage of their favourite species, write fan fiction-style books about them, and role-play Cyclist-inspired fantasies. A good place to see these oddities is at one of the several

Cyclo-cons (cyclist conventions) and sport book festivals that have sprouted around the world in recent years, probably on the back of the smash fantasy graphic novel series *Wiggins*, and the recently successful rom-com *The Cyclist in the Yellow Jersey.*

Strangely enough, you rarely see a *Cuckoo* on a bicycle. Their desires are based upon the camaraderie and style of the cyclist, though they love to make their selfies as authentic as possible! Most of all they love talking about cycling best.

DOMESTICATED
CYCLISTS

Sadly, it is not all good news of cyclists running free, frolicking on the sun-warmed tarmac and asphalt. There has been a worrying culture of cyclist servitude in Asia for a century or more, where a species of cyclist was domesticated and then bred with the sole purpose of becoming a transportation device for other species. Sadly, despite the actions of cyclist welfare campaigners, these 'cycle rickshaws' have been spotted in the UK recently. It is now believed that rickshaw stables are maintained in every major city in the UK.

It isn't know what breed of cyclist was beaten and 'broken' and tied to the saddle of these contraptions, but we believe that it must have been some variant of hardy *Tourer*, no doubt with traits from other breeds bred in. We COCKS have been active recently in an attempt to raise awareness of the conditions of these unfortunate cyclists, dragging fat tourists on city sightseeing tours, like so many beasts of burden, but sadly there is little that can be done. Tests have shown they cannot be released back into the wild, having no survival instinct left. Those who have escaped captivity are invariably found in the sewers begging for tips and offering to take passers-by to the nearest historic landmark. Shameful.

If you would like to support the fight against cyclist domestication, give money to our organisation, and in return you will receive regular email updates on our efforts, as well as our 'I ♥ COCKS' badge.

COMMON PREDATORS

The migratory routes of cyclists are full of perils, and there are a host of species that lie in wait or actively hunt these gentle creatures. This section will look at a few of the more common *Predators* that cyclists encounter on their journeys. It will be noted that in the main these carnivorous beasts prowl the more urban trails, probably due to the high concentration of prey as well as the somewhat ungainly manner of many urban species.

From the moment of leaving their roosts to their arrival at the feeding grounds, all species of cyclist will experience these dangers, and though the mortality rate is low, there are often many near misses. For the avid spotter many *Predators* will become easy to identify, though there are some (most notably the *Wheel Eater*) that will be rarely spotted, leaving only an empty carcass as evidence of their passing.

BLACK CAB

T he *Black Cab* is a fellow traveller on the roads of Britain but, due to its size and armoured steel shell, it can prove lethal for cyclists. Wholly domesticated, the *Black Cab* hates the freedom wild cyclists enjoy and therefore, consciously or unconsciously, desires to kill any it sees.

Possibly an evolutionary tributary of the *Beserker, Black Cabs* feed on apoplectic rage induced by the many perceived slights unwittingly perpetrated by passing cyclists and any deviations from its own warped misinterpretations of the *Highway Code*. It loves nothing better than swerving into the path of a cyclist as it passes, before standing over the prone carcass telling it why there are too many immigrants in the country and why it's voting UKIP.

If a cyclist spies an approaching *Black Cab*, its best defence is to stop, dismount, and wave one arm (called 'hailing'). This confuses the *Black Cab* (especially those with one yellow Cyclops eye) and forces them to stop. If cornered, many cyclists keep a rolled up copy of the *Guardian* in their backpacks, which can be brandished, causing the *Black Cab* to cower in fear of liberal views.

WHEEL EATER

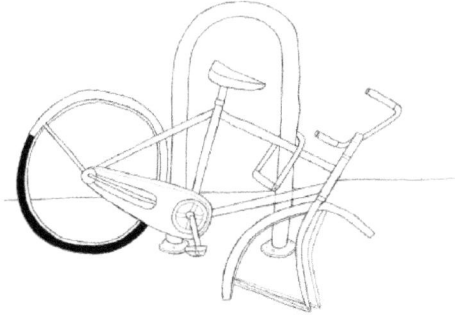

T he leftovers of a *Wheel Eater's* midnight feast can been seen in every city in the world; a bicycle, chained up near a feeding ground, mutilated, with one or both wheels missing, forks resting painfully on the tarmac. Unless help can be provided almost immediately the bicycle will begin to rust and rot, becoming bent out of shape in a matter of hours. The cyclist will enter a long time of mourning until another bicycle can be found to bond with.

A *Wheel Eater* is a figure of legend, much like a female *Trickster*, but has more in common with a *Thieving Bastard*. The only reason we know it is not a species of cyclist is because the rare and often unreliable sightings have all had the same fact in common; the *Wheel Eater* does not have a bicycle of its own. If it did have one, it would probably have eaten its wheels by now.

If you see one, please be sure to get photographic evidence and send it to COCKS for scientific research and pest control. Some-where, like Smaug, a *Wheel Eater* is sitting in a grotto atop a huge pile of excreted spokes and rims.

CANAL LURKER

As anyone who's been spotting for some time will tell you, *Wobblers* and bodies of water do not mix. Canal towpaths may seem like a safe place to migrate along, and city planners are often offering these up as safe routes for cyclists, but there is more to water than meets the eye.

When a member of the *Wobbler* genus wibbles too close to the edge of the grey-green soup the *Canal Lurker* jams a stick it in between its front spokes, before yanking the whole lot into the canal. Occasionally the cyclist will escape, bleating in panic as it drags its sodden body from the noisome waters, but it's mount is never so lucky. A *Lurker* can survive off one bicycle for many months, slowly breaking it down in its complex digestive tract.

Interestingly, the excreta of *Lurkers* are often expelled in the shape of a shopping trolley, which has led to a lot of confusion as to how all those trolleys end up in canals in the first place.

POTHOLES

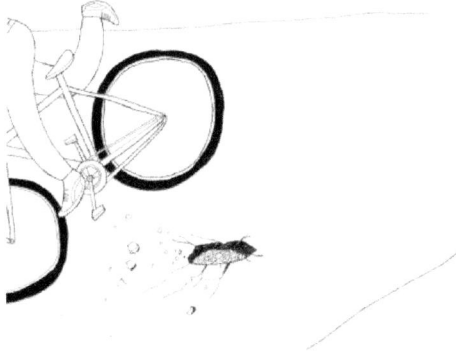

*P*otholes have to be the most common cause of injury to cyclists, and are no laughing matter.

Potholes are caused by small crustaceans called gear weevils. They burrow down into the tarmac, and create these small traps. Their aim is to jar petrol-driven vehicles with sufficient violence that a few droplets of oil, petrol or antifreeze fall into the hole and from there into the gear weevil's mouths. For the average automobile, this is only an inconvenience, but for the cyclist this can cause injury, bike death, or even death of the cyclist him or herself.

We at COCKS do not condone the videoing of cyclists hitting potholes and the carnage that follows. Any member found posting these films on YouTube will be expelled immediately.

PARKED MENACE

*P*arked *Menaces* look like parked cars, but they are altogether more insidious. They can often be seen parked in bicycle lanes, trying to funnel cyclist into streams of dangerous traffic with the explicit intention of causing a bloodbath that they can then feast on.

Another trick they have is of throwing out one of their 'door-arms' as a cyclist passes by, dismounting the cyclist. They then gorge on the resulting pile of tangled limbs.

These creatures have very small brains, and are highly unobservant, so they should be easy to eradicate. But the government so far has done nothing. In fact a sub-breed, the *Double-Parked Bin Lorry*, is paid for with government cash. COCKS is distributing a petition on this matter, which can be signed on our website.

REVERSING TRANSIT

C losely related to the *Parked Menace* but more agile, the *Reversing Transit* is the trapdoor spider of cycle predators. It will lie in wait, sometimes for hours, till a cyclist passes, before shooting out backwards from a lane, alley or covered entrance-way, crushing the victim under its rear wheels. The prone cyclist's corpse will then be dragged in through its cavernous double doors never to be seen again.

Alternatively, a *Reversing Transit* that hasn't eaten for several days may be so deranged with hunger that it will sit at traffic lights, waiting for a cyclist to pass by. When one does it will then jump the light, stopping in the middle of the road, its sliding side door gaping wide. Only lightening reactions will prevent a cyclist from launching head first in through the huge open jaws.

JUGGERNAUT

T
he *Juggernaut* is a fearsome beast, the stuff of legend for many urban spotters, though it has been known to menace some built-up areas in the early hours of the morning – most notably in the great Southern metropolises. Often identified by the roar of its engines, a *Juggernaut* is a ponderous behemoth that takes some time to build up momentum, though once it gets underway it is nigh-on unstoppable.

It has several ways of unseating its quarry. When stalking the great intercity highways that are its preferred hunting grounds, this leviathan uses a great wind to buffet the unwary cyclist until he topples under its wheels. If the roads are wet, the cyclone will be turned into a typhoon of wind and water which can blind and derail even the most athletic of breeds. The *Juggernaut* will also overtake a cyclist on a long stretch and then, reaching a hill, slow down to a crawl, its vast posterior blocking the view of an oncoming combine harvester until it's too late.

Within the confines of a city, however, a *Juggernaut* relies most on its colossal size to trap its victim, often alongside a hard shoulder barrier or against a wall. The deep guttural rumble and terrifying 'air-horn' are sounds that make every cyclist quake in fear.

Due to their sexist nature, *Juggernauts* can be derailed by female cyclists (particularly in hot pants). They invariably hang out of their cab windows to shout something utterly offensive, losing control and crashing in the process. Another technique for those cyclists being chased by a *Juggernaut* is to rip pages from a 1970s edition of *Playboy*, and cast them in their wake. Before long a centre-fold will stick to the windscreen rendering causing the beast to veer off the highway.

Printed in Great Britain
by Amazon